CHERYL LADD:

From Modest Beginnings to Hollywood Heights - Unveiling the Path to Stardom

Nathan B. Smith

CHERYL LADD

All rights reserved. No part of this publication may be reproduced, distributed, or transmitted in any form or by any means, including photocopying, recording, or other electronic or mechanical methods, without the prior written permission of the publisher, except in the case of brief quotations embodied in critical reviews and certain other noncommercial uses permitted by copyright law.

Copyright © Nathan B. Smith . 2024.

TABLE OF CONTENTS

INTRODUCTION

CHAPTER 1: INTRODUCTION TO CHERYL LADD

    1.1. Cheryl Ladd's childhood

    1.2 About Cheryl Ladd's Past

CHAPTER 2: FOUNDATIONS OF FORTITUDE

CHAPTER 3: THE START OF THE JOURNEY

    3.1 Moving to Los Angeles: The Risky Decision Made by Cheryl Ladd

    3.2 Pioneering Position

    3.3 Hollywood Navigating: Cheryl Ladd's Adventure in the Entertainment Capital

    3.4 Growth, Both Personal and Professional

CHAPTER 4: CHERYL LADD 's JOURNEY TOWARDS STARDOM: DREAMS IN THE MAKING

    4.1: Aspirations Take Off

    4.2: Calls for Casting and Auditions

    4.3: The Vacancies in the Stardom Cycle

    4.4: Leaving a Trace

    4.5: The Strength of Resilience

CHAPTER 5: EMERGING TALENTS AND OBSTACLES

CHAPTER 6: SEIZING CHANCES; CHERYL LADD 'S VICTORIES IN THE HOLLYWOOD SETTING

CHAPTER 7: LIGHTS, CAMERA, ACTION

CHAPTER 8: THE ANGELIC TRANSITION: CHERYL LADD 'S RISE TO LEGEND ON "CHARLIE'S ANGELS"

CHAPTER 9: CHERYL LADD 'S INSPIRATIONAL JOURNEY TO STARDOM: FROM MODEST BEGINNINGS TO HOLLYWOOD HEIGHTS

CONCLUSION

INTRODUCTION

Cheryl Ladd's journey is a tribute to the strength of talent, tenacity, and unyielding drive in the dazzling world of Hollywood, where aspirations are both nourished and destroyed. Cheryl Ladd's journey from impoverished origins to the heights of Hollywood fame is an inspiring story of perseverance, fortitude, and the quest for greatness.

Cheryl was raised with a strong ambition to leave her imprint on the world and a passion for the performing arts despite being from a small village. She set off on a path full of hardships, triumphs, and moments of awe that would ultimately define her legacy, all with the promise of Hollywood.

With "Cheryl Ladd: From Modest Beginnings to Hollywood Heights - Unveiling the Path to Stardom," we go on an engrossing journey through the extraordinary life and career of Cheryl. From her lowly beginnings to her quick ascent to become one of Hollywood's most adored celebrities, we reveal the unsung tales, the behind-the-scenes hardships, and the pivotal events that moulded Cheryl's path.

Using frank conversations, personal tales, and an exploration of her most renowned performances, we dissect Cheryl's persona to unveil the essence and spirit of an authentic Hollywood star. Cheryl has had an indelible influence on the entertainment business, from her breakthrough role as Kris Munroe on "Charlie's Angels" to her varied body of work in cinema, television, and music.

Beyond Hollywood's glitz and glamour, however, Cheryl's narrative is one of elegance, tenacity, and unrelenting resolve. It's a tale about perseverance in the face of extreme hardship, overcoming adversity, and standing by oneself. This tale serves as a reminder that everything is achievable if you have desire, tenacity, and a little bit of luck.

Come along with us as we travel through the highs and lows, victories and setbacks, and unforgettable experiences that characterise the extraordinary legacy of Cheryl Ladd. This is the tale of a lady who dared to dream large and whose light continues to shine brilliantly in the hearts of millions of people worldwide, from humble beginnings to Hollywood heights.

CHAPTER 1: INTRODUCTION TO CHERYL LADD

Born Cheryl Jean Stoppelmoor on July 12, 1951, in Huron, South Dakota, Cheryl Ladd is an American actress, singer, and author who is best known for her role as Kris Munroe in the beloved television series "Charlie's Angels." From an early age, Cheryl Ladd had a passion for the performing arts and pursued her dreams of becoming an actress.

Before making her debut in 1977 when she joined the cast of "Charlie's Angels" as Farrah Fawcett's replacement, Ladd's career consisted of modeling and cameos on TV series like "Josie and the Pussycats" and "The Partridge Family." Her depiction of the astute and fit Kris Munroe won her over to viewers everywhere and cemented her place in television history.

Beyond "Charlie's Angels," Ladd has acted in a variety of theatre, television, and cinema productions. Her versatility as an actor has been demonstrated by her numerous TV movies, miniseries, and feature film appearances. Her previous roles include those in "Purple Hearts," "Millennium," "Poison Ivy," and "The People v. O.J. Simpson: American Crime Story."

Cheryl Ladd is not just an amazing actress but also a talented singer and writer. Ladd has shared her experiences and views with readers all over the world via the publication of several books, including autobiographies and children's books. She has also published several albums and songs, including the popular song "Think It Over."

Cheryl Ladd has enthralled audiences with her skill, elegance, and beauty throughout her career. A star on the Hollywood Walk of Fame is among the many honors and devoted fan base she has amassed from her services to the entertainment business. In addition to her career accomplishments, Ladd is renowned for her humanitarian endeavours and commitment to charity causes. She uses her platform to use her influence for good around the globe.

Cheryl Ladd's legacy is still shining strong today, inspiring countless people with her brilliance, charisma, and unflinching attitude. She continues to be a cherished character in the entertainment industry and a genuine Hollywood legend, whether she is appearing in movies, on stage, or in the pages of her books.

1.1. Cheryl Ladd's childhood

On July 12, 1951, Cheryl Jean Stoppelmoor, now known as Cheryl Ladd, was born in Huron, South Dakota. She was the second child of railroad engineer Marion Stoppelmoor and waitress Dolores Stoppelmoor. Due to her father's work, Cheryl's family traveled frequently throughout her early years, residing in the Midwest.

Cheryl had a strong interest in the performing arts as a child. She showed inherent skill and a passion for entertaining others when she started taking singing and dance training at an early age. Even with the difficulties brought on by her family's repeated moves, Cheryl never wavered in her commitment to developing her abilities and fostering her love of the theatre.

Cheryl's family moved to the San Fernando Valley neighbourhood of Los Angeles, California, when she was a teenager. Cheryl's aspirations to pursue a career in the show industry started to materialise at this point. She started taking acting lessons and going to screen tests since she was determined to leave her mark in the entertainment business.

The usual hardships and disappointments experienced by aspiring actresses characterised Cheryl's early years in Hollywood. She attended casting calls and auditions, did odd jobs to support herself, and experienced disappointment and rejection along the way. Cheryl was unwavering in her pursuit of her ambitions, though, and her resilience and drive never faltered.

Despite the difficulties, casting directors and producers were eventually drawn to Cheryl because of her talent and personality. She started getting little parts in TV series and ads, steadily enhancing her CV and earning priceless front-of-camera experience.

Cheryl's perseverance and hard work eventually paid off. After replacing departed actress Farrah Fawcett in the cast of the iconic television series "Charlie's Angels," Cheryl received the role that would change her life forever in 1977: Kris Munroe. Her portrayal of the astute and athletic investigator instantly won over fans.

Early in life, Cheryl Ladd showed tenacity, resolve, and an unwavering pursuit of her goals. From her modest upbringing in South Dakota to her breakout performance on "Charlie's Angels," Cheryl's story serves as a motivational reminder that everything is achievable with skill, perseverance, and a little bit of luck.

1.2 About Cheryl Ladd's Past

The combination of Cheryl Ladd's varied experiences—from her upbringing in the Midwest to her ascent to prominence in Hollywood—defines her background. Her childhood was spent in the Midwest, where she was born on July 12, 1951, in Huron, South Dakota, as Cheryl Jean Stoppelmoor. As the second of Dolores and Marion Stoppelmoor's daughters, Cheryl's family experienced several moves since her father worked as a train engineer.

Cheryl's passion for the performing arts started to grow when she was younger. She had a natural gift for singing and dancing, and even at an early age, her love of entertaining others was obvious. Cheryl was determined to pursue a career in show business, even with the difficulties of moving frequently.

During Cheryl's adolescent years, the family finally made their home in the San Fernando Valley in Los Angeles, California. This thriving entertainment center was where Cheryl's dreams started to come together. She enrolled in acting school and started the tough process of auditions and casting calls because she was eager to follow her ambitions.

Cheryl encountered the usual obstacles experienced by budding performers during her early days in Hollywood. She navigated the complex world of the entertainment industry while juggling odd jobs to support herself. Her subsequent accomplishment was made possible by the tenacity she displayed throughout this time.

Following her casting as Farrah Fawcett's replacement, Cheryl made her breakthrough in 1977 when she was cast as Kris Munroe in the hit television series "Charlie's Angels." Her charm, wit, and athleticism won over viewers, and she quickly became a beloved character.

Cheryl Ladd investigated various areas of the entertainment business in addition to her acting profession. She took a go at singing, putting out albums and singles that demonstrated her range as a performer.

In addition, Cheryl wrote books, which added to her many creative achievements. These publications included children's literature and memoirs.

Cheryl Ladd's past is a testament to her perseverance, adaptability, and unwavering love of the arts. Her history is one of perseverance, skill, and the capacity to turn aspirations into reality—from the sleepy little town of Huron to the flash and glamour of Hollywood.

CHAPTER 2: FOUNDATIONS OF FORTITUDE

Cheryl Jean Stoppelmoor was born on July 12, 1951, in Huron, South Dakota, and her childhood there is where Cheryl Ladd's toughness began. Cheryl's parents, Dolores and Marion Stoppelmoor, instilled in her the qualities of hard work, tenacity, and resilience during her childhood in the Midwest.

Cheryl's love for the performing arts never wavered, even in the face of her father's career as a train engineer and the difficulties of moving frequently. She was inspired to pursue her goals and develop her gifts when she was young and fell in love with dance and singing.

Cheryl faced several challenges on her path to stardom in Hollywood. When she moved to Los Angeles as a teenager, she had to deal with the entertainment industry's cutthroat environment. Despite the several rejections, auditions, and obstacles, Cheryl's unrelenting willpower and fortitude helped her succeed.

When she was cast as Kris Munroe in the popular television series "Charlie's Angels" in 1977, she made her debut. Upon replacing Farrah Fawcett in the cast, Cheryl was presented with the challenging responsibility of stepping into the shoes of a much-loved character. She accepted the challenge, though, and enthralled audiences with her charisma, humour, and grace.

Cheryl's perseverance was seen in her pursuit of various artistic endeavours outside of her acting profession. She leaped into music, putting out albums and songs that highlighted her singing abilities. Cheryl also dabbled in writing, penning volumes that reflected her wide range of experiences and passions.

Cheryl Ladd's perseverance has served as a compass throughout her life and work. She has triumphed against hardship with poise, tenacity, and unfailing faith in herself, from her modest origins in South Dakota to her ascent to prominence in Hollywood. Many people find inspiration in Cheryl's narrative, which serves as a constant reminder of the strength of tenacity in conquering obstacles in life and realising one's goals.

CHAPTER 3: THE START OF THE JOURNEY

Determination, skill, and luck are all interwoven throughout the story of Cheryl Ladd's rise to fame. Cheryl's journey from humble origins in South Dakota to the flash and glamour of Hollywood is replete with triumphant moments, misfortunes, and unyielding perseverance. In this examination of "The Journey Begins," we go inside Cheryl's early professional life, following the critical junctures that moulded her path and paved the way for her extraordinary ascent to stardom.

Dolores and Marion Stoppelmoor welcomed Cheryl Jean into the world on July 12, 1951, in Huron, South Dakota. Cheryl was raised in the heart of the Midwest, where she learned the importance of family, resilience, and hard work. Even though she was raised in a poor environment, Cheryl showed an early aptitude for singing and dancing, charming everyone around her with her charisma and charm.

3.1 Moving to Los Angeles: The Risky Decision Made by Cheryl Ladd

The move to Los Angeles is a turning point in Cheryl Ladd's celebrity story as it signifies her audacious foray into the entertainment world. Cheryl was raised in the Midwest before her family made the historic choice when she was a teenager to relocate to the San Fernando Valley region of Los Angeles, California.

Cheryl made a big proclamation about her desire to pursue a career in the show industry when she moved to Los Angeles, which was more than just a change of scenery. Driven by a deep-seated love of the performing arts, Cheryl's aspirations of celebrity took root, inspired by the sparkle and glamour of Hollywood.

Cheryl did not spend any time getting acquainted with the lively culture of the entertainment hub of Los Angeles after arriving. She was keen to improve her abilities and polish her art, so she enrolled in acting school. Undeterred by the inevitable obstacles and rejections that came with pursuing her aspirations, Cheryl embraced the cutthroat scene of Hollywood with passion and perseverance at every casting call and audition.

Cheryl's move to Los Angeles was a turning point in her life, helping to define her as an ambitious actor and laying the groundwork for her subsequent achievements. She navigated the difficulties of the entertainment business with elegance and perseverance, encountering the distinct combination of possibilities and obstacles that characterise the Hollywood experience.

Cheryl embraced her profession with a feeling of optimism and drive, despite the challenges and uncertainty of her new circumstances. In an attempt to establish herself in the cutthroat world of entertainment, she took every chance to perform and prove herself at casting calls and auditions.

Cheryl experienced both successes and disappointments throughout her time in Los Angeles, all of which helped her to advance as an actor. Cheryl's fortitude was put to the test repeatedly, from the excitement of getting her first part to the heartbreak of being rejected, shaping her into the resolute and tenacious performer she would become.

Cheryl Ladd's move to Los Angeles was a turning point in her life, starting her transformation from an ambitious actress to a beloved figure on television. She took a daring and brave step into the unknown because she was so determined to follow her aspirations and leave her imprint on the entertainment industry. Even though there would be difficulties along the way, Cheryl's strong will and unbreakable spirit would see her through them and help her soar to the breathtaking heights of Hollywood celebrity.

3.2 Pioneering Position

Cheryl's big break came in 1977 when she was hired as Kris Munroe in the popular television show "Charlie's Angels." Replacing the departing actress Farrah Fawcett, Cheryl had to take on the challenging duty of playing a cherished character. She took the challenge, though, and gave Kris Munroe her special mix of humor, charm, and athleticism. With her depiction of Kris Munroe, Cheryl immediately won over viewers all around the world, solidifying her place in television history and launching her career to new heights.

3.3 Hollywood Navigating: Cheryl Ladd's Adventure in the Entertainment Capital

For Cheryl Ladd, her journey through Hollywood was equal parts exhilarating and intimidating. With aspirations of becoming a famous person, she moved to Los Angeles and quickly became enmeshed in the dynamic and cutthroat entertainment industry. As she carved out a career for herself in show business, Cheryl went through a wide range of events throughout this chapter of her journey, from thrilling highs to humble lows.

An important feature of Cheryl's Hollywood experience was the constant barrage of casting calls, networking events, and auditions that shaped her life. Equipped with a resolute and unwavering work ethic, Cheryl pushed herself into the competition, wanting to establish her abilities as a gifted and adaptable actor. Although she had the chance to demonstrate her abilities and attract the attention of casting directors at every audition, there was always a chance that she might be turned down and disappointed.

Cheryl persevered in the face of hardship by relying on her inner strength and Midwestern origins, despite the industry's cutthroat character. She never wavered in her honesty or confidence while going into an audition, never sacrificing her morals or integrity in the name of fame or fortune. Cheryl gained the respect and admiration of her peers for her unrelenting dedication to herself and her profession in a community where uniformity sometimes held sway.

Cheryl struggled with the demands of public attention and celebrity in addition to the difficulties of the audition process. As her reputation rose, she was thrown into the glitzy Hollywood social scene, where every action was closely watched and every mistake was accentuated. Even in the thick of Tinseltown's craziness, Cheryl maintained her sense of self and her morals, despite the attraction of fame.

Cheryl relied on her natural fortitude and unflinching will to get through the highs and lows of the entertainment business throughout her time in Hollywood. With calm and grace, she sailed over rejection and criticism, growing more resilient and powerful every day. Even though there were many obstacles in Cheryl's path to success, her unflinching faith in her skills and abilities drove her ahead and helped her reach the breathtaking heights of fame that were ahead of her.

3.4 Growth, Both Personal and Professional

Cheryl welcomed fresh chances for development on both a personal and professional level as her fame grew. She leaped into music, putting out albums and songs that highlighted her singing abilities. Cheryl also dabbled in writing, penning volumes that reflected her wide range of experiences and passions. Cheryl never wavered in her dedication to improving her technique and expanding the realm of her creative pursuits.

"The Journey Begins" provides an insight into the formative years of Cheryl Ladd's incredible career by showcasing the achievements, failures, and personal development that moulded her path. Cheryl's story, from her modest origins in South Dakota to her rise to fame in Hollywood, has inspired many people and serves as a constant reminder of the value of tenacity, fervour, and sincerity when pursuing our goals.

CHAPTER 4: CHERYL LADD's JOURNEY TOWARDS STARDOM: DREAMS IN THE MAKING

The transformation of Cheryl Ladd from an aspiring actress to a television legend served as a monument to the potential of aspirations in the making. Cheryl's journey from modest origins in South Dakota to the busy streets of Los Angeles was driven by her unyielding self-belief and her unrelenting pursuit of her dreams.

Inspired by the power of narrative and the attraction of the spotlight, Cheryl had aspirations of being a performer on stage and television since she was a small child. Cheryl's aspirations burned brightly despite the difficulties of growing up in a tiny Midwestern town; they drove her ahead and kindled a passion that would change the path of her life.

Cheryl's ideals took on a new dimension as she started her trip to Hollywood, turning from far-off ambitions into attainable objectives. Driven by a tremendous ambition to succeed in the intensely competitive world of show business, Cheryl came one step closer to realising her aspirations with each audition, casting call, and part.

But there were challenges along the way to fame. Cheryl faced obstacles in the form of rejections, disappointments, and moments of uncertainty throughout the journey; each one tested her will and tenacity. Nevertheless, Cheryl persevered in the face of hardship, finding courage in her aspirations and holding fast to her goal of achievement.

And as Cheryl's trip developed, her aspirations started to take on forms she never would have thought possible. Under the direction of her unending imagination and unwavering desire, Cheryl's aspirations grew and changed, from obtaining her breakthrough role on "Charlie's Angels" to pursuing other artistic endeavours.

Cheryl's goals continued to be the major motivator for her travels, carrying her through all of Hollywood's highs and lows. A source of encouragement and hope for budding artists everywhere, Cheryl's steadfast trust in herself and her aspirations persisted throughout the difficult and protracted journey to success.

Title for Chapter 4: Getting Around Hollywood: Cheryl Ladd's Path to Stardom

Dreams come true and go awry every day in the glitzy city of Hollywood. For Cheryl Ladd, making her way through Tinseltown's intricate and sometimes cruel terrain was equal parts exhilarating adventure and intimidating task. Cheryl experienced highs and lows along the way to fame, from the brilliant lights of auditions to the shadowy corners of rejection. The details of Cheryl Ladd's journey are examined in this examination of "Navigating Hollywood's Landscape," as we follow her path to the highest point of achievement in the entertainment business.

4.1: Aspirations Take Off

The desire that drove Cheryl Ladd to pursue her career in Hollywood was to act on stage and film and captivate audiences with her charisma and skill. Cheryl came from a modest background in South Dakota, but her goals took her across the nation to the busy streets of Los Angeles, where people come and go daily. Cheryl embarked on her mission to take over Hollywood and leave her imprint on the entertainment industry with a strong sense of ambition and a vision of the stars.

4.2: Calls for Casting and Auditions

For aspirant performers like Cheryl Ladd, auditions are the key to success and recognition in the entertainment world. Cheryl found herself traversing the labyrinth of casting calls and auditions week after week, each one offering a fresh chance to show off her skills and get that elusive breakthrough part. Cheryl went through an entire range of emotions while she battled to realise her ambitions, from the thrill of callbacks to the sadness of rejection.

4.3: The Vacancies in the Stardom Cycle

For Cheryl Ladd, success and hardship coexisted on her path to fame. Beginning her career as a struggling actor and culminating in her breakout role in "Charlie's Angels," Cheryl has direct experience with the highs and lows of Hollywood. Fame brought opportunities, but it also brought scrutiny and criticism. Cheryl had to remain loyal to herself while navigating the demands of celebrity, even as her surroundings altered.

4.4: Leaving a Trace

Amid her meteoric career, Cheryl Ladd encountered a new obstacle: creating a legacy that would endure. Cheryl had a lasting impression on the entertainment business with her legendary appearance on "Charlie's Angels" and her ventures into music and writing. Her talent and elegance inspired countless followers throughout the years. Not forgetting the ambitions that had first taken her to Hollywood, Cheryl never wavered in her humility or gratitude for the chances she had been granted.

4.5: The Strength of Resilience

A straightforward but profound truth—the value of tenacity—lay at the core of Cheryl Ladd's ascent to fame. Cheryl's resolute willpower saw her through both successes and disappointments, ups and downs, and kept her moving forward even when it looked like the cards were stacked against her. Ultimately, Cheryl's tenacity was what made it possible for her to successfully negotiate the challenging Hollywood scene and become a bright example of what can be accomplished with patience, hard effort, devotion, and a little bit of luck.

One thing is certain as Cheryl Ladd's trip to Hollywood draws to an end: getting about Tinseltown is no little task. Gracefully, resiliently, and with unflinching resolve, Cheryl confronted everything, from the brilliant lights of auditions to the shadowy corners of rejection. Despite the difficult and protracted path to fame, Cheryl's story is a tribute to the strength of aspirations, tenacity, and the human spirit. Ultimately, Cheryl Ladd triumphed, a blazing light among Hollywood's finest, her name indelibly recorded in the annals of entertainment history.

CHAPTER 5: EMERGING TALENTS AND OBSTACLES

In the vast city of Los Angeles, where dreams come true and then break equally quickly, Cheryl Ladd set out on a path that would try her will, try her soul, and lead her to the glittering pinnacles of celebrity. Cheryl experienced a flurry of possibilities, failures, and unanticipated turns of fate while navigating the complicated and frequently dangerous terrain of Hollywood; each of these events profoundly and unexpectedly shaped her life.

The Hollywood environment is unpredictable and cruel, with success and failure frequently hanging in the balance and dangerous roadblocks along the way to celebrity. In a city full of ambitious artists and actresses fighting for their chance in the limelight, Cheryl Ladd's path started with casting calls, auditions, and countless rounds of rejection. But Cheryl persevered in the face of difficulty, her strong will and unshakeable spirit keeping her going despite the failures and disappointments.

Cheryl's popularity started to soar despite the turmoil and instability of Hollywood thanks to her unquestionable brilliance, contagious charisma, and steadfast commitment to her profession. She was eager to establish herself in a field that required nothing less than perfection, so she improved her techniques and approach with every audition. She was able to secure parts in television series, advertisements, and short films as her fame developed, which helped her get closer to her goal of being a famous person.

However, there were many failures for every victory, each acting as a depressing reminder of the brutal reality of Hollywood. Cheryl had repeated disappointment and rejections, which caused her confidence to be shook but not broken. But she always bounced back from adversity stronger and more determined than before, her spirit unbroken and her resolve unwavering.

Success in the cutthroat world of entertainment sometimes comes with a cost, and Cheryl was no stranger to making the sacrifices necessary to follow her aspirations. Cheryl handled the highs and lows of Hollywood with elegance and resiliency, despite long hours on set, demanding auditions, and unceasing scrutiny. Even though there were many obstacles in her way, Cheryl never wavered in her quest for excellence, and her unflinching confidence in herself helped her get through the darkest moments.

For Cheryl Ladd, her trip through the Hollywood landscape was an exhilarating one filled with accomplishments and losses. She did not waver in her spirit or her unrelenting resolve, though, and she never wavered from who she was and what she wanted. This ultimately led to her success. Although Cheryl was about to become a household name and join the upper echelons of Hollywood society, she understood that every obstacle she had faced along the way to success had just served as a springboard.

CHAPTER 6: SEIZING CHANCES: CHERYL LADD'S VICTORIES IN THE HOLLYWOOD SETTING

Opportunities abound but are elusive in Hollywood's enormous environment; they can come in unexpected ways and leave just as fast. With every occasion, Cheryl Ladd was able to show off her skills, refine her trade, and go one step closer to her aspirations of being a famous person. Cheryl seized every chance that came her way, from casting calls to auditions, from tiny jobs to main roles, eager to make the most of every little time in the spotlight.

Cheryl's journey started with auditions, where she had to convince producers and casting directors that she was a good fit for the part. Every audition was an opportunity to bring a character to life on television, to capture their spirit and soul. Even though the deck was frequently stacked against her, Cheryl never let her fear of rejection stop her from going into each audition with unflinching confidence and resolve.

As Cheryl's career took off, she was presented with more and more options. Cheryl's talent and adaptability attracted the attention of industry insiders, leading to bigger roles in films and television series from little parts in commercials and television shows. Cheryl jumped at the chance to try something new, always willing to push the boundaries of her comfort zone and discover new creative possibilities.

But even in the glitter and splendour of Hollywood, there were times when it was difficult to find possibilities. Cheryl's path was replete with failures and setbacks as she skillfully and tenaciously negotiated the cutthroat world of show business. Rejections became a common occurrence, but Cheryl didn't let that stop her from pursuing her goals; instead, she used every setback as motivation to keep going.

The scale of the chances that came Cheryl's way increased along with her continuing ascent in stardom. Cheryl rose to the top of Hollywood's elite with her leading parts in popular television shows and box office hits, solidifying her place as one of the most sought-after talents in the business. Even though there were many obstacles in her path, Cheryl greeted every new chance with unflinching resolve and unbridled excitement, ready to grab the chance and make the most of her time in the limelight.

Opportunities are few and far between in Hollywood's constantly shifting landscape. But for Cheryl Ladd, every occasion was an opportunity to shine, show off her skills, and make a lasting impression on the entertainment industry. And Cheryl understood that every chance she had, every victory she had, had been well-earned and well-deserved as she stood on the brink of greatness, ready to take her position among Hollywood's finest.

CHAPTER 7: LIGHTS, CAMERA, ACTION

The swirl of lights, cameras, and action surrounded Cheryl Ladd's ascent to celebrity in the glittering world of Hollywood, where dreams come true on screen. Cheryl's journey from modest beginnings to breathtaking success was marked by passion, tenacity, and an unwavering will to leave her imprint on the entertainment industry.

For Cheryl, the trip started with a single flash of inspiration brought on by the draw of the spotlight and the enchantment of storytelling. Cheryl's future became entwined with the glitz and glamour of Tinseltown from that point on. Fueled by an unshakeable trust in herself and her ability, Cheryl moved one step closer to her dream of celebrity with every audition and casting call.

As Cheryl's career grew, the scope of the productions she worked on also increased. Cheryl's flexibility and talent were evident in her main roles in blockbuster films and her little parts in television shows and advertisements.

Her charisma won over people's hearts and minds everywhere. And Cheryl was ready to push herself outside her comfort zone and discover the full potential of her imagination with every new endeavour.

But even among the glitter and glamour of Hollywood, Cheryl faced her fair share of difficulties and disappointments. Rejections were a common part of her path, but Cheryl didn't let them define her. Instead, she used every disappointment as motivation to keep going after her goals. Cheryl's persistent will and overwhelming excitement were her guiding lights as she made her way through the cutthroat world of show business, bringing her one step closer to realising her dreams.

Cheryl never compromised her integrity or morals to achieve success; instead, she stayed loyal to her profession and herself throughout it all. She was glad for the chance to perform what she loved and show the world her skill, and she embraced each new endeavour with humility and elegance. And while the scene played

out on film, the lights went down, and the cameras
rolled, Cheryl Ladd's star kept rising, blazing brilliantly
as an encouragement to budding artists worldwide.

CHAPTER 8: THE ANGELIC TRANSITION: CHERYL LADD'S RISE TO LEGEND ON "CHARLIE'S ANGELS"

Few television programs have had as profound an impact on history as "Charlie's Angels." For Cheryl Ladd, being able to work on the legendary series was a career-changing opportunity that catapulted her to stardom and cemented her place as one of Hollywood's most adored leading ladies. An important turning point in Cheryl's career was The Angelic Turn, which launched her from budding actor to television icon and brought her to unprecedented levels of notoriety and acclaim.

Cheryl's path to "Charlie's Angels" started by coincidence, when life offered her the opportunity of a lifetime. When famous actress Farrah Fawcett departed the cast of the popular television show, producers searched for a new Angel to take her place. Here comes Cheryl Ladd, a casting director and producer favorite

CHERYL LADD

due to her stunning beauty, indisputable brilliance, and captivating charisma. Cheryl's career took a drastic turn when she was chosen to play Kris Munroe, the younger sister of Fawcett's character Jill Munroe. This led to the start of Cheryl's renowned role as a crime-fighting heroine on television.

It was obvious Cheryl was destined for fame the moment she arrived on the "Charlie's Angels" set. Her interpretation of Kris Munroe enthralled viewers everywhere, winning her hordes of loyal followers and propelling her into an instant celebrity. Cheryl revitalised the show with her unique combination of charm, humour, and athleticism. She gave it a new lease on life and enthusiasm that appealed to audiences of all ages.

However, Cheryl's enduring professionalism, modesty, and elegance behind the scenes were just as endearing to viewers as her magnetism on television. Cheryl maintained her composure and attention in the face of the demands of celebrity and the intense scrutiny that accompanied being a part of a cultural phenomenon. She also treated her castmates and crew with respect and decency. She distinguished herself as a real professional via her devotion to her trade and her pursuit of greatness, winning the respect and admiration of her colleagues in the field.

As "Charlie's Angels" reached unprecedented levels of success, Cheryl's fame also kept growing. Her name became associated with refinement and glitz, her image appeared on billboards and magazine covers, and her influence on popular culture was undeniable. With every new show, Cheryl cemented her status as one of the greats of television, creating a lasting impression on the industry and encouraging a new generation of actors to want to be like her.

Nonetheless, Cheryl's enduring influence on her followers—many of whom derived inspiration and empowerment from her depiction of Kris Munroe—may be her greatest legacy. Cheryl dismantled boundaries and dispelled prejudices by being one of the first female action heroines on television and demonstrating that women could be just as powerful, competent, and independent as men. Those who grew up seeing her on TV carry her legacy with them, serving as a constant reminder of the strength of resiliency, willpower, and the eternal essence of the human spirit.

Ultimately, The Angelic Turn proved to be more than simply a significant professional achievement for Cheryl Ladd; it was a life-changing event that permanently changed her course. As Kris Munroe on "Charlie's Angels," Cheryl made a lasting impression on the television industry and cemented her legacy in the annals of Hollywood history. Even while Cheryl's tenure on the show may have come to an end, her reputation as one of the most recognizable leading women in television history will endure for many years to come.

CHAPTER 9: CHERYL LADD'S INSPIRATIONAL JOURNEY TO STARDOM: FROM MODEST BEGINNINGS TO HOLLYWOOD HEIGHTS

The ascent to fame in Hollywood for Cheryl Ladd is a tale of skill, tenacity, and unyielding resolve. Cheryl Jean Stoppelmoor started her path to fame in the American Midwest, far from the flash and glamour of Hollywood. Cheryl Stoppelmoor was raised in a modest home by her parents, Dolores and Marion Stoppelmoor. Her childhood was filled with small joys and modest beginnings, but it was also infused with the virtues of perseverance, hard work, and the significance of pursuing one's aspirations.

Cheryl has a passion for the arts and a natural talent for performing from a young age. She participated in school plays, talent showcases, and local theatre performances with the encouragement of her parents, and her talent and charm soon drew the attention of both reviewers and spectators. Even though Cheryl was becoming more and more talented, her road to Hollywood was not easy, and she encountered many obstacles and disappointments.

Cheryl set her sights on a career in entertainment after high school, but her aspirations looked unattainable in the little town of Huron. Unfazed, she took the audacious choice to depart from her birthplace and travel to Los Angeles, the centre of the entertainment business. With only a dream-filled suitcase and an unwavering will to achieve, Cheryl set off for Hollywood determined to leave her imprint on the world.

Cheryl had several rejections and disappointments in the early years of her career while navigating the cutthroat world of show business. The coveted break she so desperately wanted remained just out of reach after several auditions. Cheryl persisted despite the obstacles, improving her technique and abilities with every interview that she went on.

During this period, Cheryl took on the stage name "Cheryl Ladd," which would quickly come to be associated with elegance, beauty, and ability. Cheryl immediately attracted the attention of casting directors and producers with her trademark blonde hair, brilliant smile, and unmistakable charisma, landing her several guest-starring parts in hit TV programs and motion pictures.

However, it was Cheryl's portrayal of Kris Munroe on the popular television show "Charlie's Angels" that would propel her to fame and alter the course of her career forever. As the younger sister of departing Angel Jill Munroe, Cheryl joined the group in the second season and added a new vibrancy and energy to the program, winning over viewers worldwide and cementing her place as one of television's most adored leading women.

Cheryl Ladd's journey from humble origins in South Dakota to the glittering heights of Hollywood is proof of the strength of tenacity, drive, and unyielding trust in oneself. Her motivational tale serves as a reminder that anything is achievable and that goals may come true with enough effort, perseverance, and good fortune.

CONCLUSION

One thing is quite evident when we consider Cheryl Ladd's incredible journey from humble origins to the pinnacles of Hollywood: her route to celebrity was both amazing and inspirational. Cheryl's journey from her modest beginnings in Huron, South Dakota, to the glitter and extravagance of Tinseltown, is a tribute to the strength of tenacity, drive, and unshakeable self-belief.

Cheryl had several challenges and disappointments in her career, but she never let them stop her from pursuing her goals. Rather, she saw every obstacle as a chance to develop, learn, and advance as a person and an artist. Whether negotiating the cutthroat world of show business or assuming the limelight as one of the most adored leading ladies on television, Cheryl embraced every chance with dignity, modesty, and an unwavering will to achieve.

CHERYL LADD

The encouragement Cheryl has given to countless aspiring performers and actresses worldwide, however, may be her greatest legacy. Her story is a wonderful illustration of what can be accomplished with perseverance, hard effort, and a firm trust in oneself. From her breakthrough performance as Kris Munroe on "Charlie's Angels" to her several film and television credits, Cheryl has made a lasting impression on the entertainment industry and motivated countless artists to pursue careers similar to hers.

As we say goodbye to Cheryl Ladd's amazing career, we are reminded that, despite its challenges, becoming famous is always a worthwhile goal. Cheryl has consistently demonstrated by her unyielding dedication, limitless skill, and contagious personality that everything is achievable with patience, hard work, and a little bit of luck.

Let's celebrate Cheryl Ladd, a genuine Hollywood icon, a source of motivation for all of us, and a brilliant illustration of what it means to follow your passions and never give up. May we all be motivated to aim high and follow our passions with the same unshakeable resolve and unwavering trust in ourselves as we celebrate her amazing accomplishments and think back on her incredible journey.

Milton Keynes UK
Ingram Content Group UK Ltd.
UKHW021316110424
440997UK00061B/921